vertigo

gillian harding-russell

RIVER BOOKS

Copyright © 2004 by the Author

All rights reserved. No part of this book may be reproduced or transmitted in any form or by any means, electronic or mechanical, including photocopying, or recording, or by any information storage and retrieval system, without permission in writing from the author and publisher, except by a reviewer or academic who may quote brief passages in a review or critical study.

River Books and The Books Collective acknowledge the ongoing support of the Canada Council for the Arts and the Alberta Foundation for the Arts for our publishing programme. We also acknowledge the assistance of the Edmonton Arts Council.

 Canada Council for the Arts   Conseil des Arts du Canada   EDMONTON ARTS COUNCIL    The Alberta Foundation for the Arts

Editors for Press: Candas Jane Dorsey, Timothy J. Anderson
Cover paintings by David Garneau.
Cover design by Bella Totino at Totino Busby Design.
Gillian Harding-Russell photograph by Peter Russell.
Page design and typography by Ana M. Anubis of Ingénieuse Productions, Edmonton.

The text was set in *Minion Condensed*, originally designed by Robert Slimbach. Minion is inspired by classical, old style typefaces of the late Renaissance, a period of elegant, beautiful and highly readable type designs. With its many ligatures, small caps, oldstyle figures, swashes, and other added glyphs, it is ideal for uses ranging from limited-edition books to newsletters to packaging. Poem titles are set in ITC's *Avant Garde Extra Light*, designed by Herb Lubalin and Tom Carnase in 1970. It is a geometric sans serif type reminiscent of the work from the 1920s German Bauhaus movement. Page dingbats are from Linotype's *Decoration Pi* font.

In keeping with our commitment to preserving the world's ancient forests and to the responsible use of resources, this book was printed on *Everest 80lb. text*, an ancient forest-friendly, 100% post-consumer recycled paper, by Priority Printing in Edmonton, Alberta, Canada.

Published in Canada by

> River Books, an imprint of The Books Collective
> 214-21, 10405 Jasper Avenue
> Edmonton, Alberta T5J 3S2.
> Telephone (780) 448-0590   Fax (780) 448-0640
> www.bookscollective.com

National Library of Canada Cataloguing in Publication

Harding-Russell, Gillian, 1952—
    Vertigo / Gillian Harding-Russell.

    Poems.
    ISBN 1-895836-79-4

    I. Title.

PS8565.A6323V47 2004   C811'.54   C2003-906909-5

Vertigo

Acknowledgements

My thanks to the editors of the following magazines and anthologies who published some of these poems (some in an earlier form):
The Dalhousie Review
The Fiddlehead
Grain
Let Yourself Go: an anthology of Grief and Loss (Black Moss, 2004)
Spring Magazine
Swimming in the Ocean at Night (Leaf Press, Lanzville, B.C., 2003).
Kaleidoscope

I would also like to thank Kelly Jo Burke and CBC Radio for broadcasting poems on "Gallery." "Chest of drawers" placed in the "Simply Good Poetry Contest" held by the Ontario Poetry Society "Echo Lake" won third prize in the Saskatchewan Short Literary Awards (2004).

Special thanks to David Zieroth for his editorial assistance and proofing. Thanks also to Elizabeth Brewster for her keen eye, and to Candas Jane Dorsey and Timothy Anderson for their added editorial expertise. I would also like to thank my friend Sharon Hamilton for her assistance at the end of the first draft.

Thanks to David Garneau for allowing me to use a detail from his paintings "Vortex" and "Starlight Tour" for the cover design. They are also the inspiration for the poems "(in between)" and "Belief" in the collection. Also thanks to Bella Totino of Totino Busby Design for the lively cover design.

"To be reborn one must die, Tenar. It is not so hard as it looks from the other side." — *Ursula Le Guin.*

To let understanding stop at what cannot be understood is a high attainment. — *Chuang Tse xxiii*

The pains we inflict upon ourselves hurt most of all.
— *Sophocles*

Table of Contents

I

Hard Mountain

II

Open window
for my husband who likes lilies
frictions
chest of drawers
insomniac
old guitar
She says 'it doesn't matter'
tears… the children are fighting
'I'm too tired'
Echo Lake
Untitled

III

When I have just climbed up
the trouble with blue
the trouble with yellow
the morality of colour
that the heart
voice prints i, ii, iii
voice print: omega
(in between)
Vortex
Mark
Belief

IV
No other
changeling
red fish
Lorne Street
waiting for Santa at -40° Celsius
Intersection

V
broad daylight
night vision
drifting
crossing the Ring Road
ravine
tiny blue flower

VI
Two finches: a poem in two parts
Part 1: calcium…
Part II: Plato's bird
belugas
Einstein's brain
what if…
dermatitis and the mysteries
Hathor's eye

VII

Bear #66
Rebirth
bear
Herta says
We are dirt
… if leaves be lives
without apostasy
If I could wander…

VIII

Vertigo…
half lives i
half lives ii
half lives iii

IX

back on the news (one year later)

For my husband, Peter.

III

Hard Mountain

Coming from a safe valley of life, I climbed Hard Mountain
to study cloud shapes. Midway up, among these tangled branches of thoughts
in this forest of trees unspeaking, I stopped. Walking. A thousand
eyes, unseeing, I couldn't say hello.

Watery bird notes sifting through… sounds so precise, inscrutable
speaking to me. To *me*. Their sequence liquid, diaphanous… notes floating
dazed among motes of dust in a sea of light into my swimming ears, pouring into my
naked brain (I could not retain…).

All the world spread out beneath my feet —

Rock shape cloud shape, inchoate. Shapes re-
arranging themselves, recreating themselves

Rising up this staircase of sunshine
cloud pavilions wreathing mists round and round
the mountain head with Saturn rings of pink and purple cumulus piling dreams
unravelling at breakneck speed etching lives before my eyes. As I stood there
stray memory wisps infiltrating….

Damn this lack of oxygen, spirit air!

Dizzying… even as I staged my own death,
watching my own beheading among these trees, in this theatre
of trees (with trees chopped
                              down, each day)

the scarred mountain quarry foggy, fulminating with faces, spirits
written in or breathed upon the ancient rock face

I listened…
        a jack pine felled

The north side ragged with flight and fright
        with small animals scurrying—

                …

A crow seared the mountain air
raucous hilarity melting into the seamless atmosphere
into which all thought is woven. All things that happen, have happened
been talked about, forgotten. Happened again.

Even now a bear, driven by hunger
or hate, weaving the trail…

Supremely unmoved by this inevitable scheme, unable
to cry, I watched from the safe tower of myself
Oh so lightheaded! Assailed by spark of angel,
white celestial disks floating

inside the glittering bowl of my head, I was woven into
the sky, the airy cocoon of a dream, watching myself
born again three times

…as my lover watching me, die

…as a daughter, watching her mother die

becoming that mother watching her babe
with a sword, cut in twain

helpless, watching
myself, each jittering time… I cried out!
the cracked open sobs of the earth desperate, release
with the slide of rock that drags all under—

Waking up, at last, in anguish
last wisps from the morning's dream on Hard Mountain
dissipating in the old sun's round stare, I could *not*
stop crying while I noticed the presence of dew drops
counted the remaining rays
of the sun's still long day…

II...

# Open window

It is true, the door was closed. The children safe below, building Lego towers
with arches for mechanical horses to ride through—

I opened the door as Bluebeard's wife, eyes sweeping
into the room on a parabola of updraft. Curtains beating wings
against my anxious ears. A ladder up against the window ledge
headless, looking out — two stick arms raised in alarm
at gaping air beyond all window and frame

Just this fly on the very edge, walking
along the window ledge, now climbing up the valance
against all discretion and gravity. Taking off
into the wind's hot mouth, blown in zigzag
across ginnungagap's azure seething formless   cloud fluff
overhead, brainlessly light…

It is true that I knew you were removing the screen
to this upper bedroom window. It is true that I knew you were planning
to repair tiles torn in yesterday's storm: four and twenty blackbirds
                                        ruffled on the roof top
or scattered black wings
across the lawn; but what I saw eons away

below the brainstem, and all this commotion of air
and thought, were coarse sand grains sizzling diamonds in the hot sun's glare
(protected between car and garage) watching with a thousand un-
interested eyes
                as you walked out on the tilting roof
of the world, I whispered *Be careful!*

        but you may not
have heard—

for my husband who likes lilies

I

Pale simplicity of the (sometimes
deadly) flower, whose vast sculpted white engulfs territories
underwater depths blue green, unimaginable
shades of history, purple introspection
elegant, long neck
like a chalice

fashionable satin
petals
with invisible landing stripes
for the aeronautical bee who eyes
patterns of pointillism at the dead centre
hums to 'put her in the mood.' Could it be
that bee's precise stumble

or some more accurate accident
drew him to land
aimed for clitoral antler,
stood upon
vibrating the thoracic chords
(simultaneously orchestrating
himself—

alive!) singing out the seeds
deep in the throat
of that release?

||

While some flowers, I hear, respond
only to more brutal excavation,
requiring their mates to scratch, claw, pry
grab, and rake out pollen

in which case, I'd prefer to be low-lying moss
remain staid with the wise gingko, flowerless

|||

This Easter lily you gave me unfurls
Paradise or Gethsemane on its dragon's tongue

wafts a full palate
of fuzzy aroma. Three days past

resurrection and its prime,
its sweetness will be

death's toll, I try to warn you of rotting things rolling
out its foul mouth, this yellowing

slip of discarded petals to be
more like an ancient leather glove
shrunken

with so many fingers
slipped off the bone, shrivelled up

and that aroma, subtly changed now,
that of the grave

I sometimes feel its dust on nose hairs
dappling the several passages of my throat
coughing out certainty
with life itself.

frictions

The morning slants in grey
undecided
and I am a stone; but
you turn over
pulling me into your need

all the while I'm thinking
of the youngest's sad anger at school
how to make his "b"s march ahead
instead of behind, the logic of the sullen "d"
standing against the flow
he understands better; and
the middle one's reluctance to bother

with homework; the nonsensical pressures
about what is cool the eldest must endure: all the while
you are aligning the familiar geography
of my body to your own
geography, with

the friction of earthquakes
pulling me towards some magma
not quite lost at the core of ourselves, drawing me
into the volcanic slot of your being—   I feel
your solid goodness in the breadth of your chest
that rare warmth and comfort setting off
a spark and a quiver

after-shock releases all that's
caught
frogs leaping
among the swampy sheets
in hectic waves about our heads,
and I remind myself

at least, I may change the bed.

chest of drawers

Ghost of a Sunday afternoon in March, white-washed light off
old snow is too much or too little to read this old Valentine by.
If I slant the Venetian blinds acutely upwards, shreds of light pass through—
there is no sun, just this smudge among cloud,
light's diffusion, its grayness
effacing…

Valentine of a golden retriever with a rose in its mouth
(who knows what really goes on in the golden distance
between its benevolent brown gaze?) All you know is
you want to pet the poor animal. Now
before or even after it is too late

buried inches under the children's art work
from last year's school things, on top
of half-finished embroidery belonging
to a very tidy aunt inherited inside
this chest of drawers of hers
you have never thrown out

what was once hers
(inside)
our family possessions piling up
in layers, on top

sediment ruffled up
in the wind of daily-ness, burying itself
forever

insomniac

The last of evening, a bruised pinkish
bunching over peaks, conflicting
diagonals of houses to the west
and I think of my middle son's

trouble sleeping, his meticulous
planning and counting of hours, to fall asleep
at such and such an hour, awake

refreshed for the coming race
at such another hour (eight hours sleep
you need for maximum performance, right Mum?)
sensing his growing resistance
to sleep as spirit outlives the body's needs and
something in himself unsolved outweighs

the mind's resolve; his frustration
unable to meet such fictional deadlines. "I'm tired, why
can't I sleep?" his angry protest
against the untidy lives we seem to lead
when body cannot be shut
down
like a computer.

Meanwhile the youngest drops into the cavern
of himself, even at such a noisy hour, asleep
in a moment, though the house is alive
with argument and all manner

of foolishness. Waking up
to the sun perched nimbly on the back fencepost, fierce
red eyeball blazing between Venetian slats, afterimage

of shine which through closed lids
emblazoned the brain with almighty things
a good half hour before consciousness…

old guitar
(On the anniversary of my sister's wedding – ten years after her divorce)

I find myself watching you, aware
of details, a stray fly on the fruit bowl
surreal silences
enlarged? half expecting you
to turn on me, perhaps when I am loading
the dishwasher or emptying the garbage
and you are scrubbing the pots, I jump

at silences, jarred after
you say you will be out of town
the whole week. Would you use the same voice
you used when your job was phased out twelve years ago
and we had to look elsewhere? Or like when
you were going to hospital for a test
and needed me to pick you up afterwards;

only this time would it be different?
When you come home late
from the Home and School Meeting
I've urged you to attend while
I put the kids to bed, why do I
panic? What could be keeping you?
I think of the organizers, all women
glossy and competent at the helm
you talk to so well as, tired,

I fall asleep with the kids.
Half hear you creep up the stairs
coming up from behind, touching me
with a million secret fingers, pulling
me awake. Think of

the scratched-up guitar
propped up in the corner of your workshop
like a dusty old friend, and am glad
suddenly, you have not thought
to replace it.

She says 'it doesn't matter...'

when he says he has forgotten
to phone
                she shrugs it off
...when he tells her that he was busy
chatting in the lobby, forgot
the time until it got past
calling at the time he promised
to call her at eleven o'clock
give or take half an hour
so who cares?

...where the tired man at the desk
answered her worried voice three times
he wasn't in, still wasn't in, still wasn't...

the game of cribbage with the boss' gang
went on and on talked hockey drafts and best player lists
with a dab of politics thrown in

it doesn't matter, she says
sliding into some storm cloud at the centre
of her not listening
making coffee for him
and herself
steam rising   ions, protons

neutrons swarming
invisible crossfire within a radius
at his not listening to her not

listening
within an electrical framework of wires
netting the walls around them
above the nuclear power plant of the kettle and herself
boiling fast fast

to all the details of his trip
the stupid racket in the next room
some heavy partying going on, he remarks
on broken bottles, someone crying
at the Tropical Inn

(where the tired man at the desk
answered her three times you wasn't in, still wasn't
in, still wasn't…)

steam rising rising…
from the cloud all the while
She's listening to his telling her
about the disco an ocean deep below sleep
all night long

her voice not the worried shadow
voice on the phone the deadman clerk
heard well past midnight *what could be wrong,
an accident, the car smashed…*

measuring dark spoonfuls of grounds
into the filter funnelling dregs
their daily poison/ refreshment
sparkling clear
black, rich aroma floating

"You better get some sleep tonight."

watching the tilt of his head
deferential to her sympathy.

tears... the children are fighting

"It's my turn!"
"Nerd!"

and she drops a plate
skittering across to the right-hand shelf
to start a cavalcade among the cut-glass artillery
of long-stem wine glasses.

At an eye shot, three smashed, and a flower vase
nicked, and now the toast is burning   shards
falling jagged from the cupboard above
piercing the kidney-shaped omelette
to its hidden heart.

Slanty-jowled as a jack 'o' lantern: STOP THAT
RIGHT NOW! Scraping the charcoal off
the burnt outsides; it's all
my fault your fault, toss
the toast into the garbage—

"What's the matter?" He looks up
from the newspaper.

Look what you made me do!

'I'm too tired'

She says as he turns over
in a huff

his back a boulder
between us

barrier reef sluiced through
by angry pheromones winged and nasty
fiery biting
mosquito bitten   unable to

feeling like warm, just
warm caressed, on a wolf's tongue caressing
its young or its prey
       stinging, singing, stinging
too late… this feeling

She crawls up to him, holds him between fragile wings
fanning invisible ocean torrents
(of forgiveness?)

between

the kindling smouldering
in dangerous, bare
proximity.

Echo Lake
(For Peter)

                    …on the shimmering blue waters, we are out
on a boat, capsizable

                        …in crystal light of early June, and
that silver jack fish you caught within the stillness of the lake
    slimy and slippery to me, dropped
                            into the pail

        but you told me
        it was good to eat; fried it
    for me on a small fire we built
on the un-raked shore
      beside your parents' cabin;
        tricked me into eating it
        skin and all

      …July and August, lying on the beach, your skin
the colour of sand down to the sweating green water,
                  the growing heat collecting on your brow
        beer in your hand, talking with the other
of this and that: *the fish, remember*
                      the fish!

    Laughing at something you say, unaware
of invisible letters writing themselves in the air, on the sides of the glass, drops
                  on your forehead picked up

      by a sudden wind

          out of the clear blue

            whirled round the beach

        and back —

      where one last boy among a jostling three
      makes a final dive

        We hurry to gather hamper and towels
      all the while casting glances
across the reeds and sleety blue

          towards the spectacle
of the lake
         lightning bolt spearheads the water
            where it meets   the sky

            rain drops, hours or years later
       splotch
              Splotch

(between memory of thunder
                            and torrential rains—)

The children at the wharf, now
      our own children in the back seat
  on the long drive home —

      the lake, sometimes tangled and greening
these days, shrinking or other times swelling in the gathering heat
    before thunder and
                  the rain still falling on your hair…

Untitled

Riding the swirl over the windy ravine
red on a black wing
in early May

crossing the scorching black tar of a new-laid road
the arduous passage of the caterpillar
in June

seed of an eye growing on me
(or something just past me)
its news so urgent, the yellow beak
of a crow, wide open
raw caw cawing
in July

the magpie mouthing obscenities
dragging out the guts of a small creature
living just minutes ago

the rolling miles of brown turf
down to the ravine
where the ropey branches swing

resting my head on the shoulder of a good man
rumble of his heart a steady stream
just inches beneath the rocks of ribs, the pebbles
of my cochlear ear

until cold weather
on the cataclysm of change, on the tottering edge
of this or that

and the drudgery of steps
between here and there…

III...

When I have just climbed up

      to what you had considered a solid speckled granite ledge
  looked around

    dizzying…

        scoop of air

                hawk, stoop shouldered
      riding thermal currents of elation
      the bowl of the valley, mesmerized by

a lean coyote scouting the field for mice
below

      the drop, eternity
      in a split

    second

  to rock bottom (where there would be

relief no more anxiety, this falling, falling

  the grey numbness of…

      floating molecules of unknown

potential

  or simply unconsciousness ?)

the trouble with blue

Describe the colour
blue?
at its bluest flower
or turning to turquoise of Lake Louise
turbulent with mountainous thundercloud
or the whited-over blue
of Athabaska's cascade?

Even before the dust of the thought
has left you, chicory-scented as July
fields trailing fox tails, wild oats, flax
sweet-smelling clover
the odd thistle
amongst, blue imparts,

departs…

a cloud having passed over
(So you may doubt it ever was)
You cannot, cannot conjure it up
in its exactness of hue, apart
from what it must imbue: the sky
untroubled by cloud, that distinction
or purity

in absence
before desire unleashed
evolves to a spectrum of redness
to sublimation of purple (a bloodied
blue) to tender pink
or to the flame and danger
of sunsets.

the trouble with yellow

Think of yellow
sunshine
(the first lemon air!)

mellow of butter sliding through
long afternoons…

then invisible hospital decay
where jaundice sets in
(an old light unmade
with a faint smell of pinesol)

and just tell me:
Is yellow right or wrong?

the morality of colour

To recognize red
full-bodied, silk-skinned as an opened rose
green's cool ambience and resilient long leaf

(alternatively red's matchstick of anger;
and green's mutable poison)

to recognize the differences between
when the shade to the perceiver remains
grey sameness?

to find red in the aubergine
of the bruise

to sense its shyness in the clear blue
of a forget-me-not?

Though many have seen these colours
(unidentified, in their hearts

or barely identified with shades of pleasure
or worry—)

that the heart
(for my son, thirteen years)

is (not) controlled
by the brain

has a life

(before the life)
stalking the spirit…in the shadow of its becoming
within the nimbus of a womb
first dot, igniting the crepuscular being
… to be

that the heart is a fist
four-chambered and dark, pumping
black blood through gunshot of ventricles
(such dungeon of purpose) starved *lub*
of entry, contrapuntal
dub of exit

lightning branching at the aorta
World Tree with roots… reverberating
at the wrist
a pulse

sacred temple

. . .

      that the heart is an unknown country
    resting within an enclave of flesh
sliding between silk of secretion, riding the purple horse of diaphragm
    archly, by an arresting thought
        caught (three times
denied ...)

    heart
    tucked under
    left biceps of lung
    notched for its caress

    beneath vestigial cherubic back wings
    of bone and cartilage so that you breathe faster, faster
    at the heart's address

    at the brain's blind messengers,
    the brain's radical underground committees
    say at a bald measure of song

    that calls up raw memories from centuries ago
    around the fire and in the smoke rising through the trees
    at the roots of being in the drum beat
    in the heart
    in the pit of the soul

When I swing beside the curb
to pick you up outside the school
you turn on Wolf radio, the car exploding
with "Come together right now, over me,"
and I don't say, SHUT OFF THAT NOISE!

Turn it down.

voice print i
(friend, long distance)

Hearing your voice across the miles
I am reminded of stars
dead light years

before they reach us. Their shine
redshift (your voice blueprint
wrapping long fingers round
my heart in a knot

scowling contradiction
for joy) edging

crabwise, through
the mind and memory.

voice print ii

Just as the female bat, small brown
undistinguished, flashes
into the dark
underside of a bridge, population

of babies barnacling the bridge struts
and wooden supports (she is picking up
radar

from her young ones,
buried in a forest of sounds, waiting
open mouthed, waiting for sustenance)

so I, having turned my shoulder, have lost
you among the clothes racks and three fallen-off
shirts left lying between the aisles,
(I can't pick up now!)

frantic— listening
for the thread of your voice
to pull me through all the other sounds

the lady at my elbow asking me
to describe what you are wearing, that other voice
on the intercom, it occurs to me,

might scare you away, announcing your name
between requests for price checks and
the *musik musik* and

I am calling your name
listening for your small voice
to answer me back

When the young man with the name tag
brings you to me, your face blank
tight with tears held back
full of reproach
that I might have lost you.

voice print iii
(for my godfather, who died suddenly)

I am writing letters at the dining room table
  when in that apparition of a thought
    I am thinking of you…

  (It *is* Sunday afternoon, after all
  when you used to call.)

                crystal clear

  Really you may be that supernova
pulsating light-years past extinguishment.

voice print: omega

You dragged the answering machine
thick in dust and time
out of the basement, between
the boxes of old clothes and yellowing papers, set it up
for us who didn't know how to

(never comfortable with such machines)
in the kitchen between the microwave and the fridge
This is how you use it, you said, just fourteen years old
and knowledgeable, unreeling miles

or eons of tape back
to when it belonged to Gram.
A time machine into the past with an uncle's New Year's greeting
for the coming year that happened a decade ago, and your cousin Angela
talking to a girlfriend about a boy named Preston

whom no one remembers now.
Should we erase these voices? You asked
from the past and I knew from a shadow in your voice
you had felt it too.
A ghost's blessing and the other a shiver of
déjà vu.

I think I may remember Preston now.

… (in between)
on David Garneau's painting, "Vortex"

How through the weave of everyday
tenth-of-a-second wavers
through

the scatter of habit
within the trash can of consciousness
that grab bag

to invoke this ghost
of a feeling: surreal, Uplifting
three-dimensional   focus
rising within
blur

Within the enchantment of a space
music, black hair threaded silver with shine
pulled taut

braids flowers undulating
luxuriant, voluptuous with wave
the crown of a head, or a birthing
sort of pain

the skein of a tune, unwinding
on an old-fashioned gramophone
or black hole drawing
you in, pulling
you out

of a tune, warm ecstasy
on the high wave

amid everyday
background

noise/confusion

Vortex

When a left-handed demon pulls the string
at the back of your eyeball

and the right eye
decides to see better with glasses upside-down

and the world is shunted
into reeling

your shattered glasses
shipwrecked under the breakfast bowl

at the foot of your tea cup
underwater chaos emerging misty

that biscuit shape a face you love, that hunkered
white a car through the sideways

gleaming window
a reminder you are whirling

into some black hole of dread
at the centre of which

you must drive someone
somewhere

but must arrange instead   to walk
on sunshine

smelling the earthy grass scents rising flower faces
nodding hello hello

at some faceless passerby
you recognize from the long purposeful stride

or the strutting half walk, lopsided sideways
shuffle

that is rapidly becoming yourself
with the weaker part becoming strong

and the stronger
weak

and there is no rhyme
or reason

when icy winter precedes
global warming and

apocalypse happens on the day
the baby next door is born…

Mark

Caught with your hopes up
you fall short
of the mark, tripping

over an un-
expected stair, need
another pair of eye-glasses to make
out what's wrong, can't read

the dials that say 'do this do that…'
in a foreign language
in the basement half-light
and feel you don't know for sure
anyway
while a woolly black sheep of shadow
without distinction hazing the roil of clouds
could be an ocean between heaven
and hell, and there is no telling
where the light and the dark
begin and

you have not
the stomach

for tomorrow
what lies ahead
two feet planting what goes ahead, what's
left behind to grow up, footprints in the dirt
from which we emerge
to be read
and understood or

misconstrued.

Belief
(on seeing "Starlight Tour," by David Garneau, with my daughter, 14 yrs)

…because the world lies
before me in a language thick with number against
the backdrop of a billion-faceted

digital probability
outside/inside black matter, with quantum physics and statistics proving
only in hindsight that

all is roughly unreadable—
numbers— rational or irrational— will find their precise
mark on man-made registers or will not

…because I cannot see the alphabet of atoms and molecules
nor the declensions of chemical reactions nor the parsing of chemical interactions
and because I cannot see the genes and the chromosomes
unravelling until they are
unravelled, and

the finished Child before me (alive
and separate in the sea of her own dancing molecules
sunlit around her) and I cannot see

the roar of neurons inside her beautiful head
as she tilts quizzically to regard the world
nor guess what she is thinking

until she speaks unwitting or
chooses to tell me
in part, or has acted upon
that inner roar

…and last, because the chiaroscuro of blue-marbled skies
holds no hint of the night to come (illuminated beyond
doubt) I am still not prepared

for the black alternative of night
star-pricked by distant bright hope
that a blazing sheath of archangelic Light
all-encompassing lies
beneath

waiting for the shell of the world
to be cracked open—

No other

The mother who had it all (she was a doctor,
had a loving husband
most of the time) the life
to go with it

throwing herself into the white white whirr
shining metal wheels
within

cement walls deeper, deeper
within this underground

Charon faceless
behind the hulk of the sleeping subway
shoving its imperturbable way, or beckoning…
by what weird chemistry of fate
transported through what mists of unnatural grief
vegetative fronds burgeoning brain tendrils
holding her down

down
consciousness a downer these days
(once she could lull those after-hour nerves
in a Valium sleep)

the next shift's need
to re-focus
encroaching…

Just this note left unspoken
by the phone

If only you knew

…

Gone cold turkey
chicken parts once elbowing inside herself;
now the infant outside
a living organism
nattering to be nursed

Unable to placate you, your crying
incessant, I clutch you (blind lids serene asleep
at last after an hour crying ratchety
in tune
with my need), I step

into the empty glare of noise
the rush of the world's feet, headlights
raising ghastly heads through
this snake of passage
penetrating thought in a cold damp

(... if only you had been born to me at another time, in another

World)

Think of the adoptive mother who came to her child
with the memory of the perfect child she never
had imposed on the soup cans and everywhere

abandoning this lolly head among the unholy aisles
shopping cart bogged down like a snow plough

among the bread loaves and donut packages
awaiting shelving, one box

turned on its side, smear of icing
wiped off a dozen faces, faceless
except for the gaping hole
of a mouth oh oh

oh....

*Nibble, nibble... who is nibbling
on my house* slick as fear
running across the curtains of an infant's mind

Did the undersized four-year-old among the bread loaves rising
like gingerbread houses, Nanaimo bars iced smooth as marble floors,
cakes curtained ballrooms festooned in flowers
remember *that* story?

Her real mother, guilt buried only layers
deep
in love/hate: only sixteen, never believed:
it could happen
to her

hate/love eruptive—

Give me back my child!

changeling

A toddler wanders through sliding glass doors
(left not an inch

ajar)
through the black door frame into winter
dawn (pinkish in the east

to the right) into the marvellous white-spun sugar
of snow, new fallen

outside: bitter
cold, such traitorous beauty. The child's conviction
someone can always save you
turning to fear, then

pain, and the numbing
in the neck
of despair, gone   *fiery*

Later she is found under an eight o'clock sun,
                                  blue fish—

Using all the latest medical methods,
warmed to blood temperatures;
how revived to open
doll's eyes, alert

to every noise about her
succinct (what would there be left
to fear?) everything and

nothing
as before, the mind invisibly—
touched

in its tortuous journey through a labyrinth of nerves
thawed

the fleshy brain having travelled through
districts of itself
beyond turbulence and pain (un-remembering
complexities of clouds   monstrous metamorphoses
before the red eye

of the sun, rising—)
having traversed dark skies, grandstanding it
under a placid moon and a multitude of stars
to a widening shore

the spawning banks
of an (almost) happy recovery / forget
the frostbite, skin chaffing seborrheic, allergic
to touch, blackening limbs to be lost, and
Repress…

…most lately, the ghost of frost giants icicle teeth
smudge cold thought   iron-eating limbs, half-
remembered
recreated in the twists
of an ancient, recurring
dream

red fish

Following the logic of molecules and energies amassing, dissipating,
recreating themselves from nothing when something

must always have existed; did you hear
the philosopher declared himself an atheist?

Swallowing a gift of lox from his lover, its savory tongue
plied softly upon his own tongue

he choked on the wise fish, reported
travelling down a long passage

the beautiful-veined flesh of the throat
to a cry, not of joy,
but of what?

black hole wormhole, leading
to the other side: a crowning

burning birthing sort of pain: red light
at the end of which
he must *run it*

blocked headwaters
behind uttering, spitting sizzling,
the Styx or some other
amniotic back-up

un-flowing ice, bound   in terror
sinking through a tangled forest
of consternation (how infamous to die
on a lover's bone!) so that
what he saw at that moment
was God, wasn't it?

Resuscitated by machines that rewire the requisite
body functions, closed circuits that contain
and obscure exits out of, entrances
into this world, to restore life's humming
processes. When told he had been
pronounced dead, clinically dead
for a full ten minutes,
heart stopped
brain stopped

He saw, with horror, the blue fish
of himself, eyes bulging at what origins, recalling
partly, something else   the mind
going on like the headless chicken's, spirit flailing
in an odourless ether

Now gazing into the hazel eyes
of his wife's familiar eyes, trying to remember those forests
(or was it seaweed?) just how the light
filtered through
during that mottling of becoming

How his heart hurdled over
an illicit barrier
into the infinite lap of something
glimpsed briefly

escaped,
but narrowly…

Lorne Street

With my son talking in one ear
I saw her falling behind glass, in slow motion…
stopping the car in mid-stream, mid-
thought on this almost deserted corner
inside the heart of a town.
"Don't go, Mummy!"
to that hag, ugly as a troll;
but the thud on cement
was flesh and her head.

She had flopped over stiff yellow workman boots
without laces, her mouth a widening sore
blood filling angry creases of her face, a map
of how she'd got here
so rough-shod.

"I'll get help!" I breathed by her side,
afraid to leave her, urging her to stay
still

Eyes burning cigarette holes through me
incinerating me, erratic hate flying off
the handle *of a million fears winding
tiny, futile self-propelling circles*
"I'll call an ambulance"
"No!"

She didn't give a damn if her lip was cut… Her cat!
who'd take care of her cat she had her cat
to take care of Mary beat up on her
real good lots worse lots of times
the landlady a fucking bitch trying to make her
get the hell out trying to kill her but
her brother was a healer…

"I'll call the police… you are bleeding"

The man in the Sasktel truck across the way
answering my wild-armed summoning,
reluctantly coming over…

Later she slip-walked a few blocks farther down Lorne
in her ill-fitting boots; up ahead
the grey basement apartment with the newspaper-covered eyes
bleached of all writing, just over there
maybe hers.

waiting for Santa at -40° Celsius

I rushed ahead of myself, leaving
behind myself, keeping up

to myself. The children bouncing up
Where is your scarf?
What about mittens?

Santa's coming, Santa's coming!
Calm down, calm down, I told the children
Large flakes placid molecular twinkling in smooth drifts
freeze dried in this beautiful sub-zero
I shifted from foot to foot.

Up ahead a police car in the middle of the road
blocking traffic. We parked to the right, watery lights
psychedelic staccato burbling red blue
red blue in a solid remembered column
with whiteness at the core
wiping out sight

while that lesser private demon pulled an optic nerve
behind my left eyeball, like a slingshot
I stood, my seeing catapulting

inside an elemental world   shivered fragments
distorted, viewing the world as Gerda's friend,
in the arms of the Snow Queen, but
Calm down, calm down,
Santa would be coming…

Standing beside you smiling away
from the sun's glare
reflected back on chrome, myriad crystals
sparkling in ditto

that erased seeing, I stepped over
myself (left in a heap)
feet numb
as I trod over broken glass.

So cold, large opal flakes
glittering otherworldly jewels in this ordinary high noon,
I thought of Aladdin locked in Paradise
among his jewelled trees
underground

surely the pieces of today would fit into tomorrow
and into the string of days, I struggled to think
of the day before

bobbing mechanical elves mingling with
elves on a platform floating down Ste. Catherine Street never
want to end, my mother beside me…

Ice slivered insidious
as knives inside this winter puzzle, disorienting
twin rainbow pillars
on either side of her diamond throne
I could not see past

to solve. But the children in their hot young bodies
at Santa's parade, and so I looked out
again, at the world at my feet

such a marvellous scroll of a drift
by this curb. Look! Its conch-shell formation
trumpeting godlike
as at the Gates of Heaven

. . .

with the snowbank in front of me
opening like a wave into another dream where we all lie
on a cloud bank carried in a litter across skies
with a vision of sugar plum fairies and
Wolf radio chasing the blazing sun
across the brain

Calm down, calm down

(by now as calm as snow)
Santa is coming ...

Intersection
(for my son, Laurie 9 years)

You said do you think we'll survive it, and I admit
I fumbled what had the adults said over coffee, un-rumpling
the reams of news?

I mean the snow we could be
buried under snow swirling down
round us wet flakes in april this
unusual weather we are having when

suddenly you leap into the air   broad-jump
across cement to the puddle ahead: mirage
or cancerous eye glinting black water
inside—
    a froth of snow in front
of the intersection. I see a Mazda
turning the corner

very fast, fish headlights blundering through
my arm cutting through air
between you and …
comical, hopeless   windmilling
scarecrow   signalling through splitseconds

my urgent
on a twirl of wind   cry !

uplifting   fearful knowledge to catch you, shrilly
just in time.   scrap of paper dances ahead, clinging
to grey undersides of the sidewalk across

. . .

this intersection   between worlds
invisible and   just
missed
        I feel its vibrations

activated… its black pull of space;
my charged thundering embrace
equal and opposite
angry / sad / relieved

where something almost happened
while we were just talking —

V...

broad daylight

                      The dog sees it

          (frozen)
                          whitely

       across a desert of snow; but then
                             it starts off

ha! ha!'s ! over its shoulder

  The sun ricochets off   chrome
of passing cars, bedazzling these jacks
     loose-jointed, angling off

     in a "terrible hurry"
in another direction…

      Forty below and these winterized rodents hop over
      the fallen plank
             chew bark off
  the skinny apple tree in our back yard, surviving
most of them, conveniently absent-minded

    but aware
of the dangers —   .

night vision

    I turn the corner into the night
    headlights tunnelling the dark
       empty field

    before the graveyard— level crust of snow
    white angels are leaping are veering out
      of the headlights' cowl. Exposed

      in their dalliance
          on a shining altar of snow,
                        they scamper, chaotic

    into protective shadows and darkness
    across ravines into the stubbled ditches.
       They zigzag
          crazy
                across the dark curvature of earth

    with pounding hearts, on big feet

        with sinewy legs.

      … and the night unscrambles the day in sudden
    synaptic haywire   runs—

  drifting

I walk the dog along this bike path
        extinguished by snowdrifts skirting
                diamond fringes toppling over

                                        the rolling prairie
… smooth long lines flowing oblong

                        snow

                                subliminal   *jackrabbit*

        out the corner

        (among snow swirls, invisibly
                moving through the whites
                                of eyes—)

        I *think* I may have seen something
    passing through

                the nether side of mind, just nothing
                that can be talked about
        in terms just so, as well, less
than anything…

crossing the Ring Road

The portal of God is non-existence
　　–Chuang Tse xxiii

Early Sunday morning
a moose filters through
suburban houses and fenced
backyards, across everyday
parking lots, following

a trickle of a thought
along the slough bed inside Wascana Park,
shining brown muscled back
large antlers like work-gloved hands

shovelling out space
snorting ground inside
the still sleeping city

inside the first blue
of morning prayer

The distant jogger a non-threatening target
moving at the periphery of vision
like the elongated brown shadow
of some enormous hare.

ravine

Walking over stubble grasses poking
through styrofoam snow between school yards
and winter begins again, and you are asking
why Easter Bunny hides money

instead of eggs this year for Matthew
at school; and I see it in your eye
even as I am searching
for the quick answer
to keep everyone's fictions alive
and happy

when we find ourselves arrived
the usual spot by the tree
where the path divides and
you pat the dog while

I walk the rest of the way over the dirty fringes of winter
past the slurpee cup tipped over, straw lurching over the sidewalk
behind the rows of houses along the bike path entering
the narrowing ravine before an outcrop of condominiums
(that one a sultan's dream come true!)
blocking out the sun's watery yolk
washing over the marble cornice of the building.
Out the corner of my eye, a jackrabbit
floats over the landscape brown

mottling white like a beggar's coat. He stops, sniffs
under the high wires' incessant buzz, long ears twitching
sensing some worldly change may leave him out
(a bounty set on gopher tails last summer;
they'll surely never go
the way of the dodo)

. . .

I glance at a finger-space of sky
between houses and chimney stacks
to dirty-laundry clouds
: dwindling scrub grasses
all that's left of wilderness

beneath my feet. The sex life of insects, crickets and grasshoppers
dormant in clay podsol and stinking muck; how it is
they reinvent themselves like the scarab out of dirt
come to life
at winter's end, and am comforted

to learn bacteria thrive in thermal vents
on the ocean floor, spewing out
hot gas
between creations—

tiny blue flower

Lifting leaves to peek

under
growing impossibly

in the crack
between rotting fence boards   inaccessible
with lawn mower

difficult to reach even with scissors
I could just pluck
between two fingers

remember to look for
next time.

VI.

Two finches:
a poem in two parts
(not an allegory)

Part 1: calcium...

The zebra finches peep-peeped before dawn
constant chorus not fooled by the grey blanket
we tossed on top

of the cage. They thought the dredged light
of morning sparks through fabric
the smear, perhaps, of a meteor; but I heard one singing
the other clamouring hopeful, I thought
even in the dark

ether between dream
on the peripheries of my own sleep.
We bought the birds a handicrafted nest
"So cute," you said, at the pet store; but
they tore it apart: bare ribs of basket
angled at the egg-shell ceiling
seen through bars. When the female escaped
hardly remembering what it was
to fly

the great sea distance across the livingroom,
it called out to its mate

across two rooms
dropping notes in flight
all about this new freedom
unscrambling   alphabets   in   the air—

now on the kitchen counter, against
the glass entering a safe enclave
between storm

. . .

windows (caught
between worlds). Its seeing both ways
cross mirrors reflecting/confusing
the other

the wind of furious hands;
the smoothness of a dream
about greenness outside

unreachable. She called and called through
a memory of space and freedom
Light shining through sheets of glass
(watching this and that).

When you shook loose the inside pane
she flew out   a pulse in the air
slipping out

of your hand, past
the parabola of steam from the kettle
ascending

(just escaped)

Next morning the female laid an egg,
hopped about triumphant
telling the male as they sang
together in jubilation.

I hadn't liked the idea of a bird in a cage, you'll remember—
I opened the drawer of the water dish: off-white stone of an egg
perfectly oval

I pushed back in
the amazing egg — returned with water
in a coffee lid to find

just this smash of yolk, the shell
partly eaten.

Something missing in their diet,
the vet tells us.

Part II: Plato's bird

Later we discovered the female
dived under the newspapers lining the cage
ruffling the white and black blurr
off the edge of the world.

Just a scruff of orange peak
tuxedo feathers angled for flight, wizened feet
curling under.

You tossed the carcass in the garbage
(one of the kids worried about the unmarked grave
on top of the orange peels), but the garbage truck
already turning the corner
out of sight so we returned

to watch the one bird
left standing on one leg
a wintry perch, eye
lacklustre pebble
inscrutable, fixated on us.

Someone had the idea of a mirror
(oneself is company), but even as we fixed it to the bars
the bird in a fury of recognition
knocked it into the gravel
on and off

stalagmite of droppings under the fossilized branch
randomly pocking the mirror like a window opening up the sky
beneath its feet.

As we covered the cage that evening, the remaining ruffled shape
the male's backing into the seed dish,
not laying eggs.

Next morning I lifted its sky

. . .

The bird frozen in flight
on the bottom of the cage.

And on top of the mirror
flat on the ground, an ogre's face,

pools of greenish excrement
for eyes and nose, something like, well
the man-in-the-moon.

belugas

What do those small eyes, that great head
quaint, receding gargoylish comedian forehead
see? More or less of the universe
inside or out?
At Stanley Park, the big male's quizzical eye
is a small coin tipped sideways
under diaphanous lids
fixed on me, the bystander

to get the better look. The female, less inquisitive
on the other side of the tank, calf lolling by her side
ignoring our gawking. The trainer tells us
their killer whales are gone, how the last calf
sickened, and the one before that
dying
not just an accident.

They're pretty intelligent, he informs us
while the big fish with a stick in his mouth
lures a by-standing seagull
even as the trainer had lured him
with a fish. The seagull evasive, wary
of the trick, at last

taken in. That weird, outlandish high pitch
like sudden laughter
What nuances, what shades of thought
escape our ears?

...

Six months later and five hundred
miles from the coast
under the oceanic back of a prairie sky
I peer at the mottled heavens
between everyday drapes,
through dirty glass; look for visible signs
of weather and the world
before I step out—

    a sun, a cloud
    dragon-shaped

the moon and stars scattered
in a pattern my eyes are taught
to look for

But what if I keep finding these other patterns?

        …strain to see

  the invisible

      based on a hunch

  the bird or whale
    of a thought…

Einstein's brain

Was it the lack of boundaries,
frontal lobes, lower hemispheres
one bulging continent
of cognition

with the ability to see
as through a single pane of glass
undivided

Reduce seeing
to a well-fitting glove,
touching all surfaces with a single elegant
$E=mc^2$

"There is God," you might point with your right finger
tug of your left-handed brain (reasoning
on the lower left, reinterpreted
high on the front

distilled from the elements of fact,
theory intuited and
reassembled)

closest to imagination.

what if...

...black holes are God's many mouths,
galaxies long tongues trailing words?

Creation a spiral, a postscript
of thought...
    light years after the smear
    of a star's redshift?

What if it takes a star's life
                  to reach the spark

of consciousness at the vegetative tip of Creation

    evolving tree-like neural fronds
of consciousness growing invisible electromagnetic
tendrils into the universe

    (cross-fertilizing with the many eyes
    seeded everywhere)

    What if God, like the serpent,
bites his own tail,...
        swallows his own words

    afterwards, nutrition
        for the next start?

    Does it again, fortified
    with the practice of having said it

        (once)

        again and
        again...?

dermatitis and the mysteries

I

Why one bud flowers
before the one on the branch
beside it is

beyond me. Whether the first-turned leaf's
red or gold is victory or defeat,
leaf nerves frazzled by sun's
radiance

numb

suspended in azure, un-
focussing brilliance

to become, by fire
of the sun, elixir of the seasons;
the ice creeping in
among winter's shadows and the lengthening fear…

(but the leaf turned last
gives up its grasp,
at last, too).

II

The size of a child's palm
or heart's fist clenched
this oblong of skin that burns and tickles

is lizard's long tongue licking up
the right inner arm, alternately
Frantic. Energizing.

. . .

Incapacitating. Try this
the doctor recommends. Her glassy efficiency
the eye of fish does not fool me
after three failed tries. Still

her remedies elude me. "What
occupational hazards may have led
to this?"

But my elbow saws the air, I say. The pen
less violinist's bow than compass
finding its own way, the feeling flesh half following
always trusting, fairly cautious
not far behind.

Ah! but the mysteries of life! She tosses off
with the quick brain of a cat.

| | |

Cells elongated, distorted
two or three headed and hearted, they reproduce
their own faulted selves

piling up
mass extinction
with life buried lives deep

like cockroaches lying dead under Arctic ice

or skin flowering confetti at some demon's instigating
upsetting, upsetting the delicate mechanism
production gone manic—

IV

Think of the bold cell
who ate the rest
started a new race

thriving, crawling out from under the carcasses,
rising to the toughness of unicorn
horn or proboscis?

With the burn and bite of sun and season,
it might be useful to grow scaled armour,
then shed another layer—

Hathor's eye

When the molecules of storm
invaded my brain, lying

rain-swollen among brain cells, squatters
in that fleshy compound, a torrent

began the room a whirlwind
careening on some invisible gyre

of low-flying wings, wind
and consternation

Whether it was the noisy drive downtown,
kids in the back seat, arguing,

evil demon glint
bouncing off chrome

the climb up six flights
of library stairs, a child

mischievous, behind stacks,
refusing to reappear

or just backlog
of unremovable obstacle

worthy of Ganesh— (I *had* fancied
I spotted some dark other in the underbelly of the thundercloud

over the windshield— that set in motion
that roar within

spinning the ceiling light
above me

an inscrutable eye)

while I sprawled on the floor
at the centre of worry and an idle meditation

about the nature of molecules, evolution of consciousness
Did such brain misfunction

remove the necessary illusion that the world and the universe
stand still

while we and our stars
dance and cavort ?

…that we are staggering

      cartoon characters *unfolding piecemeal*

    under time's infinite

      spreading wings—

Bear #66

    Busy eating berries among the bushes, you know
all about winter, inside of long dream as well as outside
of insufferable cold. You can slow down existence
    better than a yogi learning to survive on a single pear
        for spirit energy

        I want to name you— the name
the twins in your rounding belly would know
        you by.

        (Think better of it)

    In dreams, I have watched your tired mother
allow you to battle her, cuff her off
        tolerant as you, too, will learn to be
            some day.

Rebirth

The day the snow caved in on me
I learned no one could save me.
The long, articulate tunnel constructed from his snow fort
to my castle, I'd followed in winding curiosity
at its sculpted turns, its infinite
regress…
         stray soft snowflakes falling round me
sitting on the rim of the world
(our house a fiction ten metres
or miles away) as I waited, frozen

in wonderment, at the white, white lightness of snow
its diamond sparkle and airy possibility
hard-edged crust underneath
hidebound with moisture
near the meltdown

Suddenly, the avalanche
and the weight of the practical world coming down
about my ears (inside this crevasse, amazed
that, yes! I *was* still breathing…) The heel of my brother's shovel
butting my knee, and reminded to push, push myself out

the rest of the way, to learn to save myself, heart pounding
at this second chance
alive

The day I lost my way on a Banff trail
I learned how to disappear
down any trail that led too far
in any direction

blind stones unable to tell the trees' gaze
subliminal winnowing through cloud thought
while a rogue bear roamed the territory

The morning we heard the screamers
less than a kilometre north of Two Jack
we shivered on the cold five o'clock ground
under a flimsy tent

Just one gigantic paw rips open the sky   her voice
Enormous as thunder—

So why do I come back each summer?
The exhilaration of the climb to the top
of Sulphur Mountain? its crevice reeking
poison escaped from Hades's mouth
deep in the cave of his introspection?

Elation of blood's fast flowing,
bird's-eye viewing over it all?
heart (in a cage)
singing…

        and the feel of flying, wind running nimble fingers
through my hair…

Of course if I reach the top
the gondolas such an easy ride down, with Bear #66
safely seen through binoculars prowling the neighbouring mountain side,
two cubs in tow, in search of berries

her beetle eyes looking just past you—

I could see God, safely
from this distance.

bear

Trundles over the mountain's vast back
rolling side to side rudimentarily,
animal

among the bushes, rises on two legs
humanoid

catches a whiff of me
(red in a rainbow of smells)
in the air.

Her great paw print
a Titan's
high in the tree above me
slashing the neck of this jack pine, scarring

This is my territory…

*I see you, am not
afraid of you am walking away
from you—*

…the buffalo berries everywhere
around us

Herta says...

                she can talk to those passed away—
            It's easy, your father's over there
        in the slouch of the armchair, gin in hand
        Your mother, more proper, sitting here…

A quickness in the air, swooshing
past. *Can't you feel it?*

Like holograms, I sometimes see their faces
shine through the day, bits of themselves
caught in certain lights, shades

of thought, faces
on blank wall   voices, uncanny
real   startling, awake
corners

of the mind, their way of thinking
winnowing through, masquerading
as my own thought

*What he said, what she would
have said* flocking like birds headed south
in the mind, locking into the puzzle
of now

(backlog of memories forever
  reconstructing themselves)

Last night I woke wrestling with an old dream,
final frames fraying the edges of daylight—

                               …

only the shrill shrill agony
left to thrill… falling over this cliff's face
was part of it, rolling down

dizzily

over the mountain's shoulder, house
like a head tilted over sideways
deserted, broken
into, windows staring into the night
broken furniture   raising catatonic hands
black birds' wings

strafing the mind, impotent…
locked in itself

but there having come back
to the dream, night after night, it stops…

You see, I cannot remember
before I was born in that other dimension
either. So having entered the Light

that drowns all shadow
how would I know
what I was knowing? Remember

outside that gossamer of existence
(you still locked inside
the other world) how could I

see through dark edges of your world
blinded by Light (as I most certainly would be)
to speak, as Herta says you speak to her,

seamlessly
across worlds ?

We are dirt

we threw her ashes
into the white, white whorl of one gigantic wave
lolling tongue rolling in, unwinding
the long shore

Open conch-shell mouth—

where oceanic sands retract
ripple waves over
the roof of the world

the floor of the widening
sky   sand crystals refracting stars
in daylight rays

clamshell and periwinkle, up-tilted
in sea drift
listening with a million emptied ears

invisible rainbow of DNA
inhabiting this fleck
among grains and that fleck…

indistinguishable, sand from ashes….

But when the last wave washes in

death's warning shot
of adrenalin

(happy,
the rest of us, still to be alive)

...if leaves be lives

gone by
settling into the compost pile

to be pulled, edgewise
by the inchworm (damp crumb
by crumb)

in such an invisible line, sewn
back into the seamless soil

what of your soft-nosed cock nudging its way
straight as branches
(winter bare) into an inverted pink sky?

witless worm or Iblis
salivating fire or some venomless spit,
acid of desire

biting into hard seeds—

the closed kernels of worlds / opened
between the hurricane blood of seasons

without apostasy

That this particle and that particle are alive
in molecular rubbing, thrive
side by side

sparked by Sun
or star fallout

influence of solar flare or meteoric shadow
interception of neutrino (angel
or demon, passing invisible through
all matter)

while at a terrible distance, cosmic wheeling
within wheeling

and the separateness of particle
from particle

re-
arranging themselves…

If I could wander...

along the fringes of time
travel up a mind beam
ride a wind-string, superstring spiralling up
cathedral clouds

(maybe infiltrate a moonbeam
deflecting off
        black ice
speculate on refraction

and the discrepancy between
light arriving / departing
diffusing
        across time)

follow the parabola of a wind gust, sweeping
over probability towards
the white hot zenith
of possibility passing through the lower strata
of a sunset blanketing pain; perhaps

meet up with a pair of sun dogs
standing sentinel at the blue gates of forever
not a wrinkle in the frozen, unrelenting atmosphere
with the sun riding a golden chariot of itself
passing through the crystal air

Jack Frost juggling icicles: razor sharp points
eyeing me from among fingerprinted snowflakes,
dendrites of light, prismatically flashing—
(my human remains in a shadowy heap
below)

and if I rose ever so purposefully
to find myself in a towering White Light:
motes of angel dancing
in a perennial weather vane of birthing
and becoming

Under my feet a scudding sea of clouds hurrying across
gray and ruffled, roiling locks with a sea of faces
seen among the molten mental waves, and
treading ever-so-carefully over this sludge of faces gone by
might I recognize someone passed away
before I looked up
at the looming fog bank at the End of things?
Dare I ask whatever/whomever billowing Presence(s)
his/her/its name and ontology?
Who. Where and when. Was.
at the First Flash—
black / light
white shadow

Dare repeat the Question
until I could hear, listening
very intently to the answer mapped inside
my own evolving brain?

. . .

What s/he/it was doing
when heaven and earth, the universe   stars
meteors. nebulae of planets brewing, stewing ...and congealing

What s/he/it was doing
when heaven and earth, the universe   stars
meteors. nebulae of planets brewing, stewing ...and congealing
Begging their pardons, what had they to do with *mass*
plus gravity = zero;
the equation deflecting, defecting

                              unstable

suckling into the leakage —

5 / odd days (creative
            mistake) in the mathematical 360° circle of a year

   — — negative gravitational field
                inducing the Big Bang—

Vertigo...

Consider you are standing at the top
of the world (every point
the top), consider

that that world is spinning like a top
at 100,000 km/hr round the sun round
clusters of bodies, Milky Way
stars   synapses, if only
your brain could register,
it   standing back

far   enough   to   see

your lungs sails filling in & out
each breath driving your blood
pumped through your heart through 96,000 km
of blood rivers racing, swirling into the sea's rocky channel
Charybdis and Scylla, to be swallowed
drowned (time-lapse gene
faulted to activate— cancer or
heart attack or brain haemorrhaging— at such and such an age,
give or take a year) pituitary a promontory, directing
that chemical storm

of sea change, emotions eddying
round the cortical map of your body
your brain, the world
the universe

Consider how you have just learned
you should sleep along the magnetic poles
of the earth, head aligned to the north
of dream

(that repository
of desire and dread, the need for there to be
or not—)

...

How your bizarre, elephantine memory
might otherwise be seized to supply some
god in need

To unravel the trivial day
how your friend was telling you
he arrived at the Saskpower office tower
with a billing mix up, "wanting to talk to someone".
Employees in rows at computers behind the window:
telling the receptionist he "wanted to talk to someone…"
being told he'd have to telephone; but someone
was right there he could see her through glass.
(Feeling he might just understand an impulse
to knock someone down.)

Consider the young body-builder who would be a super hero
reluctant to step over the aged white-haired monkey
in the sauna, leering
while he refused to move over—

And the events that unleash
the day - that 'story' that couldn't be true
you saw a tower in a dream
shadowy in the brainstem, in someone else's dream
knocked down— all spinal nerve clusters
registering sense and essential human-ness   severed
with lightning surreality, glaring nightmare's radiance and fear
on technicolour TV, with anarchy and Babel
and the threatened fall of the Western world
even as the ancient city of Ur

fell you saw it from a hundred angles; heard
the wagging of a hundred tongues
on the news and from your neighbour beside you
three suicide jets bombing into the World Trade towers
and the Pentagon

the smooth choreography of destruction,
illicit beauty in the conflagration
something like fireworks, repeated shots
televised on T.V. blurring, blurring

mythologizing memory within nightmare
the grandiloquent geometry of buildings
as once pierced a landscape and civilization's symbols
crumbled to dust as, once, Ozymandias
stood in the desert

Hate as dons the devil's mask
of anonymity striking indiscriminate multitudinous
targets wields slashing knives, the gashes of a cardboard-cutter
straight-angled plumb line through the soft center of bodies— hate
as shoves resolve and the slam of levers
to make a nose dive through solid concrete
to a promised paradise on the other side
of death's uncompromising wall
Hate plated with steel, hate disciplined to operate a Leviathan, for Allah
or God, with murderous and suicidal purpose—

(Think of your own small hard kernel
of casual resentment, capable
of ferment in the dark of deprivation
and fanatic world zeal
swollen to brain size
and a twist in your soul in a predatory and unstable world
in which wholeness is tempted by the lure
of multifarious strange tunes,
and you can't identify which out of so many
the devil's tune
in the murk of uncertainty and
wanting it to be so.)

The religious ascetic mastermind
retired to the cave of his becoming,
with his secret millions commanding such faith,
orchestrating operations, a shared credit card
to finance frenetic religious purpose
among the chosen, with hate
inscribed into their lives and hearts,
their country of mud huts already torn
by war and hate unnameable, their birthright

. . .

Effigy poster of his face burns, bobbing
over the Pakistani crowds
as that country joins an imperial power in "punishment and justice"
A supporter carrying the exact poster as a banner
high over other crowds in another part of the same country,
while the wily emissary reports— "Vanished!"

Night I lie under the dome of my skull,
bursting with day's events, news items,
stories unreeling 'what ifs' racing through
the mind's asides, its takes and retakes
conflicting angels or demons
short-circuiting sleep as I become,
in turn, each casualty
I read about

Then when I am finally falling, falling.
this live spark of a fear
to whip me back

to the world's un-twirling in everybody's hands
the brain's un-mapping before blessed blackness
arrives at last

Suddenly or hours later, the shock of your hands
on the clay of my body, molding mountains, discovering caves,
all the comforting edges of the world
recovered

the Sun's terrible red eye rising
at the foot of the bed, whirling
the tight of my breath unwinding
the spinning— all select daysight would surely have edited out
the turning— beyond the ordinariness of the clock face, almost
six o'clock (too taut for yawning, I had wanted
just to sleep) then unwinding through the magic forest
of your fingers, a tangle of ourselves

Your head in my hands, and I am holding
the Sun, still, still, yes, for a moment, at least
in its turning, turning—

half lives i

Consider how solar winds in our adolescent sun flare
every eleven years; in our middle-aged sun flare
every eleven years (consider

the new improved Quebec hydro
high wires whistling over
another Babel

reaching up to the sun). Consider sunspots
solar activity, increased

expended, the magnetic path of desire
or its square root, magnified
to incineration or rarified
to absence. Consider

the rarity and regularity
of mass extinctions propelled by man/not
man

half lives ii

Consider the meteor that dashed
dinosaurs into the gloaming of an eked-out survival
forty to sixty years, the leafless crosses of trees
dwindling scrub dying in the dusty rose noon. Consider

such a giant meteor falls
every thirty million years,
any moment

to drop through the clear blue eye of day
a blood drop into the yolk of the Sun.

Consider black matter as protoplasmic
blood flowing through, filling your mind's shadows, reshaping
thought's endless half-lighted choreographies—

half lives iii

Cygnus X swirls black
unseen in the lair of darkest
intensity

Our star's blue glow 9th magnitude
circling

thread of shine peeling, un-reeling
an orange un-

    spiralling
        Light

down the drain
of the universe

Until then… .

… that that vast belly of nowadays cloud hangs
soot-ish pink   flatulent
overhanging

the narrow belt of horizon
obstructed by buildings… over the world, churning

IX.

back on the news
one year later

Osama sending tapes, not videos
this time. Voice etched on celluloid
messages sent from other where

(whether this one's a hoax
to jolt the cause: faceless demiurge
heard

terrorizing, ubiquitous
harder to locate
or part of some American plan
to drum up sympathy), and I am watching the archangel-sculpt of your lips
proclaiming threatened worlds

You point out the column.
The same photo: left hand (*his* right) raised
detonator wrist watch visible
hypnotic warmth of the leader's black eyes drawing
as Lucifer's, heat with the threat
of fire, and I am watching

the cliff of your body perched over the table's
domestic edge of the world
poring over such horrific resurrections
(surprised at some twist in my own soul, perhaps,
that I might have hoped
all along

. . .

villains so convicted and full of conviction
survive against such an unfair onslaught
of might and right and technology
and the story goes on…)

*…Everybody has forgotten the war on Afghanistan was to force the Taliban to give up
Osama bin Laden the war is over the Americans victorious but Osama's
still out there…*

I have missed what you are saying
in a time-lapse thought, untangling
all these superstrings of some (apocalyptic?)
subterranean argument— hyphenated
stops

and starts or one continuing subliminal dream thread
re-articulated…

*Osama proud of small victories in this jihad
the bombing in Bali and so on… the American ally cannot be
exempt in the shadow of its binary neutron star…* and I am drifting

into the gunshot sky with nebulous clouds
and shadings of Right and Wrong
of crusades and annihilations
of escapades and vanishings…

…so the Chinese have a space station
launching satellites to show the world what they can do while the masses starve
and Korea and Iran have weapons of mass destruction too
Now Shanghai is building the Pearl Tower to surpass Taiwan's Taipei Tower
and Babel is buried somewhere eons beneath the brainstem and my tangled tongue
in the line of instinct and survival of the fittest, emulation
and misunderstandings and I am lured
down another back alley of consideration,
that peace must be dependent on war
into a gutter, twirling
down

time warp
black hole— moment of panic last night
swirling myself
willing myself
awake…

into the void of myself
unfamiliar angle of my familiar room, my brain
an enormous eyeball

pressed by thumbs of angels or devils
pouring out a paint-box of colours
blue-green   fuchsia,
thoughts (locked
inside / freed myriad   parasitic angels or demons (misunderstood?)   let loose
from the brain stem   threatening abdication
all at once

if I persisted which way? (I was
uncertain)
                                                                    . . .

inside the dream tower, people
trapped, jumping off
one last Daedalus feeling what it is to fly
a moment before rock bottom and

my youngest son's (imagined?) call
through channels of sleep   infiltrating this dark of dream of mine
chill
under the floorboards of consciousness
flames hot from the centre
peering out, and I must get up

a mid-life red giant ball of fire,
perhaps—

My accidental hand, and
the slope of your young cherubic cheek, flickering lids
quick with violent dreams about fiery, incinerating worlds
I must put out! I must put out! (inside reflecting
the outside) amid continuations

Notes:

1. The inspiration for "*(in between)*" comes in part from Garneau's painting *Vortex*, upon which members of the Saskatchewan Writers Guild in an interdisciplinary exercise were called upon to write poems. I was particularly drawn to the textural and sensual qualities in that large-canvas painting. Also I found the energy and upheaval suited my theme in *Vertigo*. A detail from this painting is used on the front cover, thanks to David Garneau.
2. *Belief*: In Garneau's painting, I see a starry sky framed by a cross-section of slightly ominous daylight cloudy blue. The artist describes his painting as inspired by an incident when police officers left two intoxicated aboriginals at the edge of town in the middle of the night during sub-zero weather, and one of the victims, an adolescent of seventeen years by the name of Neil Stonechild, froze to death. I have interpreted the painting more freely. The frame of ominous marbled white representing the acres of frozen land hidden by night I have interpreted as suggesting a larger daylight surrounding our night and mortality. Perhaps these are the very feelings and insight/delusional thoughts Neil Stonechild might have experienced while lying on the snow, hypothermic and on the brink of death.

Gillian Harding-Russell's first poetry collection, *Candles in my Head* (Ekstasis, 2001), balances precariously on a theme of birth and death as her third child was born ten days after her father's death and two days before his birthday. Her poetry, articles and reviews have appeared in many journals, on CBC radio, and in several anthologies. After earning a B.A. in English Literature (Hon.Ist Class) and an M.A from McGill University, Montreal, she completed her Ph.D. in Postmodern Canadian Poetry at the University of Saskatchewan. She has taught at the universities of Saskatchewan and Regina, has been a reader for *Event*, the Douglas College Review, since 1986 and has been poetry editor since 1988.